# UPDATED
# COUNTRY

# UPDATED COUNTRY

LIEZEL NORVAL-KRUGER

PHOTOGRAPHY BY
CRAIG FRASER

NEW HOLLAND

Published in UK by
New Holland Publishers (UK) Ltd
London • Cape Town • Sydney • Auckland
24 Nutford Place, London W1H 6DQ

Originally published in RSA by
NK Publishing in 1999, 18 Wargrave
Road, Kenilworth, Cape Town

Copy Editor: Ellen Fitz-Patrick
Art Director and stylist: Liezel
Norval-Kruger
Assistant stylist: Holger Schutt

Reproduction by Hirt and Carter
Printed and bound by Tien Wah
Press, Singapore

ISBN 1 85974 612 8

# C O N T E N T S

# INTRODUCTION

As we enter the new millennium, we live in a time of rapid change with runaway developments in technology and a massive communication overload. We are so over-stimulated, many of us have a strong urge to return to a simpler lifestyle in tune with the rhythm of nature. Our surroundings can control and change the way we feel. Spending time in the country inevitably makes us feel refreshed and energised, which is why we have always longed to surround ourselves with elements that reflect a simple, relaxed rural existence. Traditionally, country style meant a display of worldly possessions – cosy cluttered rooms with an abundance of frilled and piped soft furnishings and bunches of dried herbs and flowers suspended from the ceiling. These days, we prefer a more stream-lined look that's relaxing on the eye and easier to maintain. Clutter and fancy decorative finishes have given way to clean, understated interiors. What distinguishes this new approach to country style is an honest mix of simplicity and sophistication which results in a contemporary, yet classic interior. Decorating

*The new approach to country style is an honest mix of simplicity and sophistication*

is all about putting together interiors that make you feel good. *Updated Country* is quite simply a visual celebration of the new attitude in country decor with practical tips and advice to help you achieve the look. It also proves that a tiny house and budget does not pre-clude serious decorating. With a little resourcefulness and by making the most of what you have, you can turn any room into a visual feast. Country style decorating is inspired by a melting pot of ideas and cultural influences from around the globe. The most well-known country interiors must surely be those of English country cottages with their laid-back comfort and romantic charm. The distinctive styles of Tuscan and Provenciale farmhouses reflect the warm tones of the earth and a rustic aesthetic. Mediterranean country style draws inspiration from open landscapes bathed in brilliant sun-light and the deep blues of the ocean. Their interiors have an inherent simplicity with clean lines, stark contrasts and basic furniture. The cool elegance of traditional Swedish country style and the honest simplicity of

American Shaker interiors have an understated sophistication that are consistent with the updated interpretation of country style. Different influences have led to many variations and interpretations of country style ranging from soft romantic florals to rustic simplicity. The fundamental values which underpin the different styles, however, remain the same. In *Updated Country* I have picked out eight of the main looks in modern country décor: Rustic, Romantic, Fresh Floral, Modern Rose, Monotone, Natural, Nautical and Creative Colour. For each of these styles I have attempted to show you an interpretation of the most important living areas of the house – the sittingroom, diningroom, kitchen, bedroom and bathroom. The luxury of having a different space allocated for each function in the home is definitely something of the past. In the modern home where space tends to be limited, your kitchen often functions as a diningroom, leads off your living area and acts as

a playroom. These areas are now designed to become practical work areas with space for reading, doing your finances or maybe even incorporating a home office. Your bedroom should be the ultimate refuge – a place of serenity where you can cast off the stresses of everyday life. Pretty bed linen and soothing colours create a truly restful and relaxing environment. In an increasingly frenetic world, bathrooms have grown in importance as havens for quiet reflection. Bathing is no longer simply a cleansing routine, it is a way of reviving and relieving daily stress. You may not live a simple life, most of us certainly don't, but walking into a home decorated in an updated country style will make you feel as though you do. Fabrics, wallpapers and accessories are sourced from Biggie Best. However, this book is about ideas, rather than specific products. The updated country style can be created with a multitude of different fabrics and furnishings, available from almost any fabric house.

Today's country style is not about creating a fussy, chintzy country cottage, but more about inviting

nature into your home with honest materials and a simplicity of design. You cannot always put a price

tag to beauty. Driftwood found on the beach or the colour of wheat fields reflected in a decorating scheme probably have more value than the latest fashion innovation. Contemporary country furnishings are

# UPDATED LOOK

welcoming and comfortable. It is more about the feel of a fabric rather than the way it is styled. The emphasis is also not on slavishly trying to match up every item in the room, but all about casu-

ally mixing different shapes

and textures in an honest, natural way. Make the most of what you have by

finding new uses for existing pieces of furniture and don't be afraid to update the look. Get rid of the clutter and make room to live life to the fullest.

# Nature

The longing for a country lifestyle is all about the need to slow the pace of life and get in touch with our natural instincts. Houses inspired by nature are those in which you can relax. Take inspiration from the beautiful shades of green in an undulating landscape, the sun-bleached whiteness of sea sand contrasting with the velvet blues in the swell of the ocean and the faded yellows of ripened wheat blowing in the wind. The colours, textures and patterns of nature have the pulse of life and an intrinsic honesty, reminding us of a time when man still lived close to the earth. Wood, stone and sand are more satisfying to our senses than synthetics, and contribute to a greater sense of well-being. Modern country furnishings are made from natural materials and have a simplicity of line and a sturdy, practical grace. Pure cotton bed linen, cashmere throws, knitted cushion covers, distressed wooden furniture, hard-wearing canvas and smooth pebbles picked up on the sea shore all add a richness of texture and create a harmonious environment.

# Simplicity

Modern country decorating is about creating a serene, relaxed environment with quiet lines where form and function are equally important. Furniture and accessories reflect the simplified, streamlined philosophy. Elaborate curtain treatments have been replaced with flowing reams of fabric hanging simply from curtain poles on rings or tab headers. Pattern, like floral print designs and checks and stripes, are used with restraint, and mostly as an accent. Lightly textured wallpapers are almost plain, in pale and earthy colours. Cushions are trimmed with buttons, natural fringing or tie details, and sofas and chairs have simple loose covers. Wooden furniture has a solid, rustic appearance, a plain design and distressed painted surfaces to add texture and interest. Accessories should be used selectively and kept to a minimum.

# Lifestyle

The new look in country style decorating takes inspiration from the essence of rustic living – it is not merely a decorating style but a set of values, a way of life. Family values, friendship, caring, comfort and repose are all part of this quality lifestyle. The modern approach is to create a home where the mind, body and spirit reconnect. Our sense of touch is acute and is directly linked to our feelings. The taste and colour of food enjoyed in the company of good friends stimulates our senses and creates an exuberant attitude to life. Earthy shapes and textures bring the simple and uncluttered lines of nature into your home, while natural light brings out the true shape and character of a room, and is as important as the decorations within.

Allow the past to live by creating an atmosphere of unspoilt rustic homeliness. Take respite from the artificial pleasures of town and get in touch with intrinsic values and an  honest existence close to nature. Blend old and new objects for an interesting mix and an understated, rustic aesthetic. Layer tweedy woven checks and hard-wearing cotton canvases in warm earthy tones. With an eclectic collection of furniture that bears the mark of time, you can create a home with character and a thrown-together, mellow charm.

RUSTIC

# Sittingroom

Comfort and cosiness define this rustic style, but the look relies on an unerring eye and disciplined order to give it a contemporary edge. Bulky sofas and easy chairs dressed in layers of earthy woven checks give an inviting sense of informality. Keep the colours subdued in dirty whites, sludgy blues and greens and muted terracottas. Distressed wooden furniture and textured wall finishes are absolutely crucial to the look. Distempered walls in warm tones create an appealing backdrop for wood and terracotta. Use accessories like generous-bellied jugs that double up as vases for loosely arranged bouquets.

**clockwise from top left** *Go to markets and auctions to hunt down stylish wooden furniture that's worn and comfortable. Time-worn texture adds character and a spirit of the past to provide a context for contemporary touches such as jute- and button-trim scatter cushions and simple curtain treatments.*

# Kitchen

Rustic country kitchens are warm and friendly and the real heart of the home where dogs, children and visitors congregate. The all-in-one sociable kitchen with a spacious eating area has replaced the formal dining room. Mixing the functional with the decorative, it is the perfect space for work and play. Crisp formality and symmetry are shunned in favour of casual comfort. Dinner plates, table linen and cutlery are housed and displayed in an antique dresser placed conveniently close to the table. Visit junk and antique shops often to build up a good selection of antique crockery and cutlery, or raid your mother or grandmother's cupboards for any unwanted pieces. The beauty of old china is that it mixes and matches effortlessly. Although cupboards and dressers are the perfect answer to hide any clutter, open shelves

**left** *Use empty wall space cleverly with an antique coat rack. Sunhats, worn jackets and walking shoes or boots are easily accessible for an impromptu ramble*

**clockwise from top left** *Dressers and open shelving built in alcoves in the wall provide useful storage for kitchenware.*
*Grow herbs in pots to have easy access to fresh flavours.*
*For the best salads make dressings with extra virgin oil, freshly squeezed lemon juice, chopped herbs and garlic.*
*Invest in a simple metal chandelier for cosy candle-lit dinners.*
*Cloth-covered books add a nostalgic touch.*

can be practical and decorative. Arrange displays of condiments, screw-top glass containers, crockery and other kitchen equipment. Grow herbs in terracotta pots on windowsills and use them as aromatic table decorations. They are also incredibly handy to have at arms-length when cooking. Stick to rustic wooden furniture that has stood the test of time. Don't worry about matching styles perfectly as different shapes and colours of old oak and Oregan pine live together comfortably. Use woven check fabrics to make informal loose covers for chairs or tablecloths or to line the backs of old dressers.

# Bedroom

Textures are central to the attractively simple character of this rustic country bedroom: terracotta wallpaper, sisal carpeting, a plain cotton rug, sturdy furniture and simply hung woven check curtains. An exquisitely crafted patchwork quilt gives the bedroom traditional but unfussy charm. Despite – or rather because of – the eclecticism, this room has a particular harmony and synergy. Creating this look in a city dwelling has become easy now that the essential accoutrements of country style are easily available

from decor shops, chain stores and fleamarkets. For an authentic effect, search for distressed pieces of furniture at markets and antique shops. Choose your furniture with a multi-purpose in mind: a wooden chair can function just as well as a bedside table; a blanket box provides storage and also doubles-up as extra seating or as a coffee table in front of a sofa.

**clockwise from top left**
*Combine pure cotton bedlinen in plain creams with warm woven checks in earthy tones.*
*The fussy look of old-fashioned quilts are updated with subtler, simpler designs.*
*Put attractive pieces of left-over fabric to good use by tying documents together or to replace ribbons when gift-wrapping.*
*Well-worn furniture has lots of character and combines well with earthy, woven checks.*

# Bathroom

This bathroom is given instant character and style with a free-standing basin featuring strong masculine lines and contemporary, elongated taps inspired by a traditional Victorian design. A small mirror with a dark wooden frame simply hung with a jute cord adds contrast and nostalgia. The bathroom is spare and orderly, with fittings and accessories carefully selected for their simplicity and intrinsically pure design. Washing should always be a sensual pleasure, so indulge in refined soaps with warm, spicy fragrances such as sandalwood. Add a luxurious touch with embroidered pure cotton hand towels.

**right**  *The warm scent of sandlewood enhances an atmosphere of unspoilt, rustic homeliness.*

# RUSTIC

*Oriental Ivory*
Plascon EPL 312

*Molucca*
Plascon EPL 175

*Brittle*
Plascon B14-6

*Desert Sunset*
Plascon EPL 180

*Aztec*
Plascon C5-6

*Burgundy*
Plascon EPL 428

1

2

32

**clockwise from left** *Surround yourself with warm, spicy colours for an interior that radiates earthy comfort and style. No country kitchen is complete without the aroma of freshly baked breads or pies. Collect old silverware to mix with antique china. Keep them shiny by wrapping individual pieces of cutlery in tin-foil when not in use.*

*Look for accessories with style and character such as distressed picture frames. Make cushions with simple tie details: cut and sew a plain cushion cover of 45cm by 45 cm with an inner flap like a pillowcase. Make four ties with a finished width of 2.5cm and a length of at least 15cm. Pin the ties 1cm inside the opening, spacing them equally, and machine stitch several times for strength. See pages 156 - 157 for fabric details*

# e l e m e n t s

3

4

5

Heighten the senses with the calmness and simplicity of natural, neutral colours and textures. Blur the boundaries between inside and outside by embracing the tones of wood, stone  and earth. Explore the richness, variety and intrinsic beauty of naturally-occurring materials. Surrender to whites, creams, grey-browns and biscuit shades to reflect an atmosphere of space and light. Roughly painted wood, heavy woven cotton fabrics, delicate muslin and furnishings with a practical elegance create a restful style in tune with the rhythm of nature.

N A T U R A L S

# Sittingroom

The neutral tones of white, cream and biscuit create a graceful, restful sittingroom. Contemporary touches include simple, painted wooden furniture, plain loose covers for chairs and sofas as well as pure white vases and bowls with clean, fluid lines. Complement the look with understated window treatments such as this soft-structured blind. If you prefer curtains, choose simple tab or tie-tab designs and hang them from a wooden or wrought-iron rod. Ties, tabs or other imaginative headings are a feature in themselves and work best in plain fabrics. Be careful to steer away from elaborate finial designs. Anything too ornate will jar with the atmosphere of natural simplicity. A basic neutral colour scheme is versatile and well-suited to modern living. Its flexibility, offers potential for introducing other colours with the use of flowers or decorating

**right** *Contrast the homely feel of rough, worn wooden surfaces with clean-cut shapes and smooth textures for a thoroughly modern feel.*

accessories. Try introducing black in the form of script-design fabrics for a graphic, modern feel, or add scatter cushions and throws in spicy brick and mustard for a more earthy result. With a natural interior there are a variety of choices when it comes to flooring. Explore different materials, from quarry tiles and limed oak to sisal and slate. Wood provides warmth and refinement, while slate and terra-cotta add roughness and texture. Ideally, walls should be painted in matte white or given surface interest and warmth with textured wall-papers or ragged paint finishes in natural or earthy tones.

**clockwise from top left**  *Modern yet comfortable settings need large-scale sofas in simple styles. Invest in accessories with clean lines such as these understated limestone bowls.*

*Collect bits and pieces from nature and make displays in bowls or picture frames.*

*Loosely tie cotton rope around basic white candles to make simple displays.*

*For interest, opt for brown textured and striped wallpapers.*

# Diningroom

This diningroom reflects a spartan simplicity reminiscent of medieval monasteries. The windows are left unadorned, allowing light to flood through. Keeping them free of curtains or blinds gives an added feeling of spaciousness and the changing light adds to the atmospheric effect. The only luxurious touch is the cream cotton tablecloth that falls all the way to the floor. For a more rustic look, paint the cotton with an oil-based interior paint, then machine-wash to crackle the paint and let it form a textured,

mottled effect. Hunt for understated utilitarian tableware with pleasing shapes. Some of the best designs of plain white or cream china can be found inexpensively at department stores or even certain supermarkets. Add to the atmosphere by mixing white china with plain glassware like glass hurricane lamps or night lights in small tumblers.

**left** *For an unforgettable feast try making fresh pasta at home. Making pasta dough by hand is simple and produces a far superior result. Simply break 3 eggs in a mound of 300g flour on a smooth, warm surface and slowly incorporate with the flour. Knead the dough until it is uniform and leave in the fridge for at least 20 minutes before rolling it out. Remember that homemade pasta is best when enjoyed with simple sauces. One of the best must surely be Pasta Alfredo: put 45g butter and 250ml double cream in a pan and bring to the boil. Stir frequently until the cream has reduced by half, add a pinch of nutmeg and salt, throw in the pasta and toss with a generous helping of freshly grated parmesan cheese.*

# Kitchen

Natural and painted wood, stainless steel and plain cream cotton fabric are combined in a kitchen that is both rustic and modern. The clutter is contained in a tall cabinet with chicken mesh doors lined with cream curtains to create a layering of tones. Make use of a hanging wall system and butcher's hooks for a practical and aesthetic way of organising cooking utensils and dishcloths. If you are unable to source a ready-made version, try assembling something similar from whatever is available at your local hardware store. A good alternative are ordinary bathroom-rail brackets and a piece of wooden rod.

**clockwise from top left** *Simple everyday glass tumblers have an instrinsic beauty of their own and look particularly good when grouped en masse.*
*The well-worn surface of this old table was left untouched to preserve its pleasingly weathered texture, but the base and legs were painted white for a clean, crisp look.*
*The aroma and texture of food is as much a part of the character of a kitchen as the decor.*

**clockwise from top left**  *Give softness to spartan simplicity with a simple muslin drape. Choose jacquard bedspreads for their luxurious texture. Add atmosphere with candle holders arranged in neat rows. Mix natural finishes such as distressed wood and jute trim with the clean lines of wrought iron. Make reading enjoyable with comfortable seating. White and cream combines perfectly in a natural scheme.*

# Bedroom

To create an intimate atmosphere with softness and comfort, a simple wrought iron four-poster bed (previous page) is teamed with soft, sheer muslin curtains allowing diffused light to illuminate the room. The bed is simply dressed with a plain cotton canopy with broad ties, and accessorised with bulky bolsters so that it forms the focus of attention in this spacious room. The inside of the canopy is trimmed with narrow ties to secure the canopy to the bed-frame. Natural equals pure – a theme carried through in this bedroom with a minimum of decoration. Everything is kept simple, from the bed-covers to the dado-rail. Be sure to invest in good quality, pure cotton white bed linen and soft wool blankets in shades of cream to add a luxurious touch. There are all sorts of beds that suit the natural look. Limed wood, wrought iron or a plain divan doubling up for sitting and sleeping, are just some of the options. If you have an existing bed that does not quite fit with the look, consider dressing it with a plain cream loose cover. Add detail with a pleated skirt and tortoiseshell buttons.

# Bathroom

Create your own soul-soothing haven with a bathroom that radiates freshness and simplicity. The spare lines of this bathroom bring an air of serenity to a quick dip or longer linger in a roomy slipper bath. Subdued neutrals, simple window treatments and understated furniture allow light to become an important element. A bathroom cabinet with glass doors is ideal for storing and displaying crisp white towels, toothbrushes and delectable toiletries.

*Fresh Cream*
Plascon B14-2

*Tapioca*
Plascon G377

*Oatmeal*
Plascon WAA 5

*Mushroom*
Plascon G375

*Camel*
Plascon WAA 8

*Quartz*
Plascon BBO 514

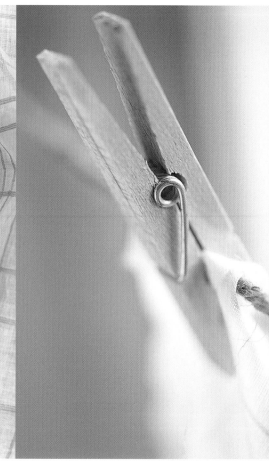

1

2

**clockwise from left** *Nature is filled with colour but the true natural palette includes an understated range of creams, grey-browns and biscuit shades.*
*Collect pebbles and interesting seeds from nature and display in wooden or lime-stone bowls.*
*Ordinary wooden clothes pegs make a fun alternative to the usual curtain clips. Clip plain lengths of sheer fabric to natural rope or thin wooden rods for beautifully understated curtain treatments.*
*Make the most of the magnificent colours and shapes of autumn leaves by displaying in frames. Crumple up ordinary white or cream paper for a textured backing and cut to the required size. Stick your chosen leaf on the brown paper using double-sided tape or glue and place in a wooden or distressed finish frame.*
*Keep detailing simple with plain button, natural cord and simple tie trims.*
*See pages 156 - 157 for fabric details*

# e l e m e n t s

3

4

5

There is something about soft, sun-mellowed English garden roses in pale pastels that is both nostalgic and marvellously romantic. Give a breezy, open feel to your surroundings, and make your home a restful  place — much like being in a country garden. Surrender to soft creamy pastel roses rambling up tea and cream backgrounds — a design classic that never fades. Give florals a contemporary feel by combining with simple shapes, clean colours and understated accessories for a look that is fresh, charming and serene.

ROMANTIC

# Livingroom

Traditional English rose designs are given a new lease of life and a thoroughly contemporary edge when teamed with a simple, neutral palette of white and cream. Clean, understated lines play up romantic curves and soft floral fabric designs. The emphasis is on natural textures, with selective floral accents in the blinds and accessories. Make the most of limited space with unusual, creative room layouts. In this instance (previous page) the sitting and dining areas have been combined. The elegant white-painted table is the focus of the room with living spaces created around it. The footstool provides extra seating space and doubles up as a coffee table in front of the sofa. When the diningroom table is not in use it acts as an area for displaying books and china, or as a convenient working surface. The overall effect is modern and tranquil.

# Kitchen

In the kitchen an old wooden table is used in combination with a selection of mis-matched chairs (junk-shop finds) for a cosy feeling of child-friendly comfort and homeliness. Antique pine is great because it is already worn; a few crayon marks won't ruin a table. The look is given a soft romantic edge with simple floral cushions, a scalloped roman blind and an eclectic mix of kitchenware.

**clockwise from top** *Collect fine china with floral designs from antique shops or rescue unwanted pieces from relatives. Store the crockery in open shelves or dressers to show off their charms but do not treat them only as showpieces. Turn every day into a special occasion by using favourite cups and plates daily. Floral table cloths give an instant lift to the breakfast table. Buy lengths of fabric from end-of-rolls or discontinued lines and hem for inexpensive and quick throw-overs.*
*An old enamel colander makes an effective fruit bowl.*

Fine porcelain cups with sweet floral designs are thrown together with distressed metal canisters and old enamel teapots. If you like, dress the chairs with tied slip covers or floppy pancake seat cushions. Be sure, however, to use fully washable cotton, as kitchens require a lot of cleaning — especially if there are children around. To keep the look light, mix painted and lime-washed wooden details (such as the baby high chair and food cabinet) with darker wood. Promote unused chests of drawers and dressers from the bedroom to the kitchen to create freestanding storage space. Give them a face-lift with a coat of paint or special effect. Stick to white walls to provide a clean backdrop for more fussy, nostalgic touches like the window architrave hung with baskets, dried flowers and strings of garlic. White-painted walls are effective in making a small room look big, and a dingy room bright.

**left** *Decant cereals, rice, coffee and other dry foods into metal and glass or china canisters for an attractive storage solution.*

# Bedroom

Tones of cream and pink can create a clear and calm mood which need not be frumpy – just steer clear of frills and keep it understated. Confine your scheme to a backdrop of white or cream and accessorise with floral touches. A modern, romantic and ultra-feminine retreat is created with a white antique cast iron bed, a luxurious ecru jacquard bedspread and a gauzy sheer muslin blind that is simply rolled and tied up. For a more structured look, consider roman blinds with plain or

**clockwise from top left** *Add a romantic touch to ordinary flip-flops with artificial rose posies. Dressers provide unusual, practical and decorative storage for clothing and personal items. Give romantic florals a new look by using them sparingly against a backdrop of white and cream. Dressing tables are given character with informal displays of favourite things. A small bench makes an informal and effective side-table.*

scalloped edges. The walls and all the furniture are painted white. White paint not only provides a serene background, it also unifies an assortment of flea-market furniture. Make sure that old paint or varnish is stripped off properly with sandpaper or stripping solution before applying a fresh coat of paint. A small wooden bench acts as a side table with black and white postcards simply nailed to the wall above it. Architectural detail is added with a white wooden dresser which is used for storing clothing and linen. Give it a personal touch with favourite things and family photographs.

# Bathroom

Light a candle, have a glass of sherry handy, put on your favourite music, and indulge in natural, fragrant pleasure by throwing freshly picked lavender or rosemary sprigs into a steaming hot bath of water. Then sink back and relax with a good book. A steel bath rack with bookstand is the perfect answer for keeping reading matter dry and storing soaps and bath oils in antique bottles. Look for an old roll-top bath and combine it with wooden floors and white-washed wooden furniture.

THE RAINS CAME

ve alone fat out
at was, he knew,
litary habits there
people were always
ble to avoid friends
always open. There
self in to be alone.
of leaving Ranchipur
was far too ill.
with difficulty, by Bates,
ke and that his Lordship
at the illness was nothing.
edicines she had taken
to him, trying to remember
he house in Hill Street,
not wakened properly. He
a comber," and now that he
anaged to take his temperature,
above normal.
that he has one of these Eastern

afraid at all. You hope he has,"
a great effort she said, " I suppose
I don't know whom to send for or

note to Her Highness, I could send

t and then write a note. Go along,
t."

face and set her hair in order and
e better, although her brain still seemed
on-wool, and when she raised her hand
as if it did not belong to her.
had gone into his room, and for a moment
ast red-carpeted Victorian bedroom tempted
otesquely, in a vast bed of teakwood orna-
other-of-pearl, and the sight of him filled
se of shock and distaste. It was as if she
operly before—how gross, how heavy he was
re half-conscious, the spark, the vitality, the

energy which had always animated all his great bulk and turned
mere weight into strength was gone, and he appeared dull, inert and
heavy, the hard line vanished from his jaw, the muscles of his big
face all flaccid. He had suddenly become simply a repulsive mass
of flesh.

And then she remembered a little vaguely what had happened the
night before in the palace and the quarrel that had taken place in
her bedroom, and she was filled suddenly with shame and a loathing
for herself, not because of Ransome or even because she was pro-
miscuous—she felt no shame for any of the adventures she had had
outside marriage—but because she had lived for nearly ten years
with this gross mass of flesh which lay in the bed of teakwood and
mother-of-pearl, that she had yielded herself again and again to him
with indifference. All the other men—all of them—had at least
been beautiful in one way or another, and she thought at once of
Ransome and how different his body was, how slim and hard in spite
of all his drinking and dissipation. Looking down at Heston she
thought, " Whether he lives or dies I'll never sleep with him again."
But she wished shamelessly that he would die, for she knew that as
long as she lived she would always see him thus, betrayed by his
illness, heavy, gross, purple-faced, with his mouth hanging open a
little ; and each time that she saw him she would remember that she
had prostituted her fine slim body to him again and again. Only
with him, her husband, had she ever been a prostitute. With all
the others there had been pleasure and even sometimes love. Heston
alone had ever paid her.

Leaning over the bed, she knew that Bates was watching her,
dankly curious to see how she would behave, and she knew that
she must put on some sort of show which, although it would probably
not deceive Bates, would make him believe in her good intentions.
She was aware that in his servant's way he already knew too much
about her.

She said, as if she were a devoted wife, " Albert ! Albert ! It's
Edwina." The dull pale blue eyes opened a little way but they only
looked into space, far beyond her, without focusing. He made a
faint grunting sound and the eyes closed again. A second time she
tried with no more result, and then she said, " I'll write a note,
Bates. We'd better send it off at once. I'll bring it to you. You'd
better stay here to watch."

In her own room she took out her writing-case and a bottle of

*Nu Buck*
Plascon C10-2

*Clay Dust*
Plascon C8-4

*Winter Berry*
Plascon C6-5

*Melon Slush*
Plascon C4-6

*Salamander*
Plascon D18-4

*Boston Fern*
Plascon D19-6

1

2

**clockwise from left** *Pink and green, exquisitely matched in nature are the perfect colours for romantic and restful interiors.*

*Give traditional floral designs a new lease of life by choosing simple, un-fussy window treatments. Distressed wood and white painted wicker emphasises the feeling of lightness.*

*Scratch around at markets and second-hand stores for old faded rose prints. For a relaxed look, prop them up on tables and dressers, or if you are after a bit more formality, group them on the wall. Ensure that your house is always filled with masses of voluptuous roses by planting rose bushes or climbing varieties in the garden or in terracotta pots.*

*Collect delicate antique china with floral designs for just the right mood.*

*See pages 156 - 157 for fabric details.*

# elements

3

4

5

Be inspired by clean, sleek lines, open spaces and the lucid quality of individual colour to create an environment radiating relaxed modern sophistication. Get hooked on graphic patterns and

architectural shapes mixed with classic and natural touches like sisal carpets, chairs with rush seats and woven cotton fabrics. Sparse use of furniture, woven stripes, subtle checks against a plain backdrop and minimal accessories create a grand yet restrained impression.

M O N O T O N E

# Livingroom

The sophisticated look of this living area, which incorporates both sitting and dining, is linear and spare. The sense of space is maximised by keeping the colour scheme and furnishings very understated. The almost abstract quality of the room is emphasised by the strong lines of the bold striped tablecloth and furniture is minimal for dramatic impact. Though furniture is sparse, it is an interesting mix of different styles: country style ladder-back chairs with rush seats, classic loose-covered upholstery and an elegant white painted console. Typical of a modern, pared down approach, furni-

**clockwise from top** *The white paint finish of the console table accentuates its fluid, elegant lines. Choose muslin curtains to create an understated atmosphere. Muslin gives a softness to contemporary curtain treatments such as tab header designs.*
*Chairs with rush seats add texture and a natural touch to the scheme. Use generously proportioned chairs with convenient loose covers to accentuate the scale of the room.*

ture has multiple functions, like using the dining table for eating, working and reading. Sheer curtains allows filtered light to illuminate the space. A muslin curtain looks best when it has sufficient fullness to show off its soft, easy-drape characteristics, but that does not mean that you have to resort to frilly finishes. Try tab-header curtains with inverted pleats, positioned to correlate with each tab, or make curtains with a heading tape of your choice and attach to curtain rings by the means of knotted ties. Keep accessories to the bare minimum and stick to black and white prints and etches in black wooden or aluminium frames.

# Kitchen

Balance functionalism with aesthetics in a kitchen that is a perfect blend between modern and country. Simple stripes and checks contrast with warmer touches like the collection of kitchenware displayed on open shelving. This kind of shelving is inexpensive yet effective and can easily be knocked together in an afternoon if you have the time and basic tools. Alternatively, get a carpenter to make them up.

**clockwise from top left**

*Smooth white ceramics lend a modern touch to the country kitchen.*

*The striped paint effect on the wall is boldly graphic but also gutsy and fun. The wider the stripe the more up-to-date the look.*

*Overhead pendant lights in spun aluminium provide a pool of light to subtly illuminate working surfaces.*

*Make the most of natural ingredients at hand by experimenting with different focaccia toppings. Chop mixed fresh herbs and sprinkle on the bread with crushed garlic and coarse sea salt, or cover with a layer of roast vegetables and shavings of parmesan cheese*

# Bedroom

An assembly of clean-cut furniture and finishes is used to create a look that is uncluttered but not stark. The mood is mellow with a soft two-tone mix that is easy on the eye. Brick and cream checks are warm, laid-back and elegant. The design of the wrought iron bed is very simple, allowing you to dress it up or down with soft furnishings. Give an interesting twist to traditional four-poster curtains by hanging them from curtain rings instead of directly onto the bedframe. Let the curtains drape to the floor or tie them back simply and effectively with a hemmed length of contrasting fabric. Understated window treatments keep the focus on the simple yet sumptious bed. Leave the windows bare or dress them with plain roman blinds.

**opposite** *Homeliness without excess is the secret to the tranquil simplicity of this bedroom.*

# Bathroom

A colonial roll-top bath, gold plated taps and shower mixer, and lavishly draped shower curtains transform a functional bathroom into something more elegant and luxurious. The curtain is decorative and practical, lined with a layer of white plastic to protect it from steam and splashes. Details like the delightful metal soap tray on the shower pipe give that added touch of luxury and make this room a haven after a long day at work.

**clockwise from top left** *The elegant shape of the roll-top bath with ball and claw feet forms an unusual contrast with rough sisal carpeting.*
*Bathing is certainly one of life's most rejuvenating pleasures. Enhance the experience with fragrant bath oils and salts.*
*Introduce Scandinavian blue to the brick and cream colour scheme to add an understated sophistication.*
*Add a refined touch with white embroidered waffle-weave towels.*
*Japanese house shoes are a must to slip your feet into after a relaxing bath.*

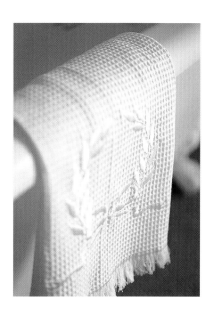

*Antique White*
Plascon VEL 6

*Rice Paper*
Plascon VEL 45

*Wharf View*
Plascon D33-2

*Mosaic*
Plascon D34-4

*Inca Red*
Plascon B4-6

*Mod Red*
Plascon PHC 4

1

2

**clockwise from left** *Red, cream and Scandinavian blue bring and air of sophistication to any interior.*

*Add effective stripes to a country kitchen. You need: water-based white paint; red glaze; varnish. Step by step: 1. Measure the wall width and divide it by the number of repeats. 2. Apply two coats of white paint. 3. Mark stripe spacing along ceiling edge. Drop a plumb line from each mark and pencil in the stripe edges. 4. Mask off the edges of the stripes. Using a broad brush and red glaze, paint the stripes, wiping the painted area with a soft cloth before it dries to form a textured effect. 5. Apply a coat of varnish.*

*Hanging buckets are an innovative storage alternative for vegetables and fruit.*

*Add interest to a dining chair with a pancake cushion with criss-cross ties.*

*A checked border gives a plain cream runner a graphic effect.*

*See pages 156 - 157 for fabric details.*

# e l e m e n t s

3

4

5

Celebrate the visual pleasure of a generous burst of deep red velvety roses with their heavy, sweet scent and delicate texture. The dramatic sophistication of shades of dark pink, red, green and mustard are perfect for modern, bold rose print designs. Elegant woven jacquard fabrics, streamlined furniture, textured wallpapers, quirky decorating accessories and touches of dark and distressed wood give a fresh look to things past and present, and creates an effective, sensual and seductive interior.

MODERN ROSE

# Sittingroom

Traditional rose-print designs take on a new identity with boldly painted large scale motifs in strong colours. These new floral prints are best displayed against a sober white backdrop or given added impact with textured wallpaper. The daring combination of robust rose-patterned curtains, clean-cut upholstered furniture, dark wood and warm terracotta wallpaper epitomises a relaxed contemporary mood. Be sure to steer away from too dark a hue on the walls as this will only subdue the impact and up-to-date effect. Accessorise with quirky touches such as small oblong cushions and the pure lines of shapely vases.

# Diningroom

In this diningroom, a bold floral curtain is set against the understated appeal of white tough-and-groove and a lime-washed timber floor. This combination with luxurious touches like silver and crystal, create a look that is modern, sophisticated and elegant. Simplicity of styling is key to the look, with the gilded and crystal accessories sparkling against a backdrop of crisp white table linen. You don't have to spend a fortune on expensive linen to create this look. Buy a few metres of white or cream cotton fabric and sew up a simple tablecloth. Add a broad border with mitred corners in the same fabric for a finished look. The extra weight of the border will make the tablecloth hang beautifully.

**clockwise from top** *Lay the table with heavy silverware, mismatched antique fine china and crystal glassware.*
*Broad, plain centre borders adds a linear touch to bold floral design curtains.*
*Introduce a touch of luxury with rich woven jacquards.*

# Kitchen

Combining utility and aesthetics, this kitchen has been designed with traditional touches, yet the end-result is clean and modern. An all-white palette is given a bold splash of colour with a simple floral tablecloth. Keep the look uncluttered with clever storage and minimal accessorising. The cream painted console table with a convenient bottom shelf provides a simple form of open storage for pots and pans, while the tall dresser with chicken mesh doors makes a feature of blue-and-white crockery. The folding chairs are a clever space-saving alternative to fixed or heavy wooden furniture and can easily be stowed to create more space, or moved to other rooms when extra seating is needed.

**clockwise from top left** *Add colour by making simple displays with fruit on white china plates.*
*Have a piece of pegboard cut and frame it in a modern steel picture frame for a handy and attractive display option for cooking utensils and pans.*
*Antique blue and white china gives a stylish edge to any decor scheme.*
*Ensure a clean and uncluttered look with plenty of drawers and cupboard space.*

# Bedroom

In this bedroom the essence of modern romanticism is captured with the combination of simple clean lines, touches of softness and bursts of bold colour against a white backdrop. Keep the look understated with contemporary floral-lined curtains – they allow a hint of floral without overpowering the room. Window treatments are often underestimated, which is a pity, because the right window treatment can transform a room, emphasising the effect of natural light and expressing a particular style. The curtains in this modest country bedroom have simple tab headers, but a fuller curtain with a ruffled edge and fabric ties fixing the curtain to a curtain pole would also work with this decor scheme. Be sensitive in your choice of curtain treatment. Make

**right**  *Mix traditional frilled pillowcases with clean-cut modern styles like Oxford borders or narrow tie details. Use contrasting fabrics to accentuate the design and provide texture. Small gingham checks work well with large scale floral designs.*

sure that the selected style suits the particular fabric you have chosen and the dimensions of the window, and fits in with the style of the interior. Rich brocades made up in elegant pelmets and formal tie-backs will look out of place in a country-style interior. Luscious layers of bedding and simple frilled pillowcases give a sense of comfort and homeliness. Contrast floral-print bedding with crisp white sheets and a white or cream comforter. Choose a wooden white-washed bedstead to create a fresh, modern effect. Darker wooden elements can also be introduced into this scheme very successfully, but the end-result will be a smarter, more traditional look.

**clockwise from top left**  *A predominantly pastel pink and blue palette of traditional rose print designs are traded in favour of more saturated hues of dark pink, red, green and mustard. Use textured and trellis design wallpapers to add a backdrop of colour.*

*Look for contemporary accessories with a floral theme. White embroidered bedlinen provides a simple base for layering with floral bedcovers.*

  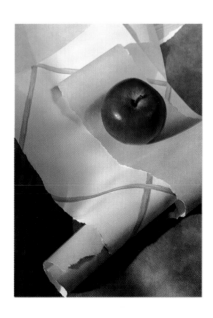

# Bathroom

Pleasure meets purpose in this bathroom with a generous view through the window, allowing contemplation of the garden while you are soaking in the bath. The free-standing bath is shielded on either side by two shower curtains suspended from simple wooden screens. A shower is an invigorating wake-up call in the morning and excellent therapy against the stresses of the day at night. Invest in a good shower system – the best have a powerful delivery and a big shower rose to evenly distribute the water. Bathroom floors need to be splash proof – waterproof wooden floors by sealing the joints and coating the entire floor with yacht varnish.

**clockwise from top left** *Finely tuned taps are essential to regulate hot and cold water.*
*Fragrant soaps incorporating loofahs are great for a gentle exfoliation with a creamy lather. Use loose-standing soap dishes to drain water off soaps so they last longer.*
*The separate areas of the bathroom are demarcated by the shower screens.*

*Rich Papaya*
Plascon VEL 76

*Tandoori*
Plascon C4-7

*Radicchio*
Plascon B4-7

*Eland Beige*
Plascon BBO 4

*Flo's Chair*
Plascon D19-4

*Philodendron*
Placon D19-5

1

2

**clockwise from left** *Green balances red and dark pink accents to create a boldly elegant interior.*

*Distressed wooden frames take on a double purpose as room dividers and shower screens. Use metal hooks or fabric ties to fix the shower curtain to the screen.*

*Leave walls white or add colour with wallpapers in saturated tones.*

*Borders give a neat finish and decorative interest to pillowcases. The correct method to make an oxford flap cushion is to attach a separate border with mitred corners. However, there is a quicker way if you are not using a contrasting fabric: 1. Make a simple square cushion cover allowing extra width for the required depth of the border. 2. Measure in from the edge the required depth of the border, draw a square and sew along this line. Play with quirky accents such as small oblong cushions.*

*See pages 156 - 157 for fabric details*

# e l e m e n t s

3

4

5

Take inspiration from the sea and create an atmosphere of true relaxation all year round. Explore the creative potential of tactile elements; dazzling colour and weather-beaten texture from the seashore. Revel in the blues of the ocean and  sunbleached whites teamed with beachcombing spoils to capture the style of simple seaside living. Hardwearing canvas fabrics, generously proportioned furniture, white tongue-and-groove walls, yacht inspired decorating accessories and rope detail create a look that is unaffected and truly refreshing.

N A U T I C A L

**clockwise from top left** *Fabric colours can change a room as much as the paint.*

*For a backdrop of colour use brick, terracotta or large trellis wallpapers. Don't worry about matching cushion covers with the rest of the furnishings, it is much more interesting to try out similar but contrasting fabric shades.*

*Accessories made of natural materials add texture to bring life to your surroundings.*

# Sittingroom

A casual, relaxed atmosphere is created by mixing comfortable loose-covered sofas with wicker and distressed wooden furniture. Both stylish and functional, the navy upholstery is the perfect background for understated, contemporary cushions with button and rope detail. The dresser, with layered white paint finish, is an ideal way to intergrate storage with the overall style of the room. The predominantly blue and white theme is given added warmth with splashes of mustard. Nautical artifacts are spread across the white painted mantlepiece and coffee table. The way you display favourite things is all part of creating order and giving your living space a characteristic look. Use natural elements to create simple displays such as stacking pebbles from the beach and filling shadow boxes with shells and other bits and pieces from the shoreline.

# Diningroom

The simple but effective look of this diningroom hinges on the play of textures. Natural tones of ecru and mustard are contrasted with black metal, unfinished wood and distressed finishes. An understated nautical touch is created with stylish loose-covered chairs featuring rope detail, simple metal hurricane lanterns and bundles of rope informally tied to a chunky metal rod with seagrass twine. Look for old maps at the archives of the City Council or yacht club for interesting but cost effective wall hangings.

# Kitchen

A comfortable, cheerful kitchen with a utilitarian feel is created with a mix of old and new. The convenience of the present is combined with a nostalgic love of the past. Create a homely feel with chairs of various shapes and contemporary touches of stainless steel and galvanised metal for contrast. Many collections and personal bits and pieces help to create an atmosphere of sociability. Seek

**clockwise from top left**

*Contrast the clean look of woven stripes with the warm, homely feel of antique furniture.*
*Eating is one of life's sensual pleasures. Simply stuff salmon trout with parsley, garlic and butter and place under the grill.*
*Bags with tie openings are practical, look good and are incredibly easy to run up on your sewing machine at home. Collect shells from the beach and glue or sew them onto bags.*
*Chickenmesh cupboards are a practical and decorative way to display china or groceries.*
*For a homespun feel with an updated edge, use galvanised metal buckets to contain lemons or grow herbs.*

out old knives with bone handles at antique shops specialising in cutlery and silverware, collect basic white plates and simple glass tumblers. Simple displays of old kitchen utensils suggest confident cooking and appetising meals to be eaten at leisure. Storage solutions are the key to creating a well-organised kitchen. An old storage cupboard can be given a facelift by the addition of new doors, in this case chickenmesh ones. Large dressers are incredibly useful for housing plates, glasses, herbs and just about any other kitchen paraphernalia. For an unfitted kitchen, combine a minimum of built-in elements (a sink, stove and worktop) with simple freestanding cabinets and tables, The great advantage of an unfitted kitchen is, of course, the fact that the cabinets and cupboards can be taken with you if you move house.

**opposite** *Collect shells, pebbles and other bits and pieces from the beach to devise interesting displays on windowsills and small tables.*

# Bedroom

Different tones of blue, from chambray to steel, lend a seaside air to this bedroom. The airy feel is enhanced with fresh looking walls: apply matt white paint to the lower half of the wall and cretestone to the upper portion above the dado. A space saving tub chair is ideal for reading and relaxing. If you prefer a more natural look, introduce a wicker chair – it mixes well with a nautical theme and is a good alternative to an upholstered chair. A small limewashed table replaces the usual bedside table creating a casual effect and doubling up as a practical work area. When not in use, you can display decorative boats, pebbles and toiletries.

**left** *Bring a jaunty touch to the coastal theme with fun objects such as small boats in bottles or lighthouse pencils. Add a personal touch with a selection of blue and white leather trim photoframes.*

# Bathroom

This spacious bathroom features the delicious textures of fluffy white towels, natural loofah and smooth pebbles picked up from the seashore. The convenient shelves next to the fireplace are covered with a roman blind — made with panels of canvas in contrasting tones to create a flag-like effect. The walls and furniture are in tones of white to provide a clean backdrop for strong accents of navy blue, mustard and brick. To enhance the look, buy toiletries in blue and white packaging, see-through glycerine soaps and accessories in natural stone.

**clockwise from top** *Display bath oils and body lotions in blue bottles on open shelves, or keep within reach on a steel bath-rack.*
*Attach hooks in a row on the wall to create hanging space for sumptuous bathrobes, towels or clothing.*
*Tones of blue, white and sand create a serene effect in this nautical bathroom.*

*Hazy View*
Plascon B31-3

*Denim Wash*
Plascon A31-4

*Sault Blue*
Plascon B30-5

*Holden Lake*
Plascon D31-5

*Cold Blue*
Plascon C32-6

*Night Swim*
Plascon B30-7

1

2

**clockwise from left** *Blue, the colour of sea and sky, is the dominant colour in a nautical decor scheme. Blue is peaceful and refreshing, generating a sense of wellbeing.*

*Choose sofas and chairs with clean, understated lines and cover with plain, striped or checked canvases. Compliment the look with black and white photographs or prints in white-washed frames, or simply nail them to the wall.*

*Rope and eyelet detail give a distinctly nautical feel to chairs, footstools, curtains and blinds.*

*Look for typical nautical accessories such as boats, lighthouses and blue stripe and check cushions.*

*Add atmosphere to the bedroom, bathroom or diningroom with basic hurricane lanterns. They also look great dotted around the garden on a sultry summer evening.*

*See pages 156 - 157 for fabric details*

e   l   e   m   e   n   t   s

3

4

5

Bring to life the heat and heady fragrance of a long, late summer afternoon with colours that are refreshing and modern. Indulge in abundant bursts of flowers and the distinctive  scents and flavours of seasonal crops flourishing in the garden. Let a warm summer breeze blow through your home with the use of sunny yellows, restful greens and lavender blues. Slip loose covers onto your chairs, dress up with understated floral curtains and throw in a touch of wicker, metal, painted wood and gold for smart summer living.

FRESH FLORAL

# Sittingroom

The atmosphere of a room is determined by the colour scheme. Rich yellow, green and blue floral designs mixed with canvas fabrics in blue and cream, create a fresh, sunny decor scheme. Although traditional floral patterns are an important element of this look, the total picture is by no means fussy, sweet or pretty. The secret is keeping it simple: pure shapes, streamlined furniture, natural elements and understated styling. In this sittingroom the yellow textured wallpaper brightens up the look, while wicker and whitewashed wood add a contemporary touch. Deciding on whether to wallpaper or paint your walls can be a tough decision. Paint is easier as most people can do it themselves. You can also get a beautiful result quickly and touch up any mistakes. When choosing your colour you must remember, however, that your result will be influenced by the wall's underlying colour and reflected light. If you are after more than just a plain colour, wallpaper is definitely the answer – unless of course you are particularly talented with a brush

**clockwise from top left** *Woven throws in slightly faded greens and yellows are handy to drape over a sofa or chair or to cover your legs while reading.*
*Stick to plain accessories with subtle details to create an unfussy look.*
*Wicker furniture is eco friendly and work well indoors and outdoors. Cushions provide a layering of pattern. Choose simple designs with contemporary trims such as natural or jute cording and button and tie details.*

**clockwise from top left** *There is nothing like the combination of wicker and the colour green to evoke images of a summer garden. Combine with trellis wallpaper and tapestry cushions for a colonial touch.*
*Look for interesting handpainted pots and fill with potplants.*
*Botanical accesories in metal adds an eclectic feel.*
*Handpainted shadow pictures with topiary designs work well against textured wallpapers.*

and have plenty of time and patience. With wallpaper you can get anything from textured finishes to stripes, geometric patterns, trellis designs and stencilled effects. You can get an immediate impression of how wallpaper will look before you hang it and it will cover up most imperfections on the wall. When deciding on a particular wall treatment or style of room, you must remember that it will largely dictate the style for the rest of your home. You need to consider the flow of pattern and colour from room to room. If you choose a completely different style and colour for each room it can be unsettling and uncomfortable to live with. Wall and flooring colours and surfaces should be as near in tone to each other as possible to make a uniform base to work from.

# Diningroom

Summertime tables draw inspiration from sun-drenched gardens with shades of green and yellow mixed with a touch of blue. Table settings should not be elaborate. Use basic white china, well-made glass and stainless steel elements for a crisp modern look. White china is a sound investment as it looks good against any colour scheme and always makes food look appealing. Give diningroom chairs a refreshing summer feel with long, pleated floral and stripe loose covers.

**clockwise from top** *Add a decorative touch to jars of preserves by covering the lids with fabric rounds.*
*White china looks good against distressed white or dark wood.*
*Steel containers bring a contemporary feel to the table.*
*An inexpensive way to build up a good selection of china is to keep your eyes open for discontinued lines.*

# Kitchen

Diversity in shape and texture enlivens the decorating scheme of this kitchen. Yellow and green checks, trellis design wallpaper and botanical prints are mixed with more rustic elements such as wicker and black metal. Avoid clutter by stacking stylish wicker baskets, the ideal hide-away for your batterie de cuisine. Baskets are also ideal places to store fruit and vegetables – which have a better flavour when kept at room temperature. Try the old Italian custom of lining up tomatoes on the windowsill in the sun. Apart from being decorative, there is nothing to beat the mouth-watering taste of sun-ripened tomatoes.

**clockwise from top left** *Keep spices organised in a distressed wooden spice rack.*
*Look for interesting accessories with a botanical theme - it is a great way to add colour and pattern.*
*Olive oils infused with herbs and spices are fantastic to cook with or as a base for delicious salad dressings.*

# Bedroom

With a yellow palette and splashes of white and gold, this small bedroom is turned into an elegant yet informal retreat. Sumptuous layers of bed linen and a floral-print fabric with a yellow summer rose-motif were used to create a fresh, welcoming atmosphere. White painted distressed wooden furniture and wreath design textured wallpaper adds a clean, modern touch. Look for existing pieces of furniture such as a redundant console table or chest of drawers to take on a new role as dressing table.

# Bathroom

Create tactile and visual pleasure with a mix of the refined and the countrified, the traditional and the contemporary. A classic floral-print curtain and stipple stripe wallpaper are combined with the rough texture of unfinished whitewashed wood and clean-cut metal trim to create a look that is both classic and modern. Hand towels are kept neatly rolled up in a delicately hand-painted enamel bucket. Similar pieces can be found in second-hand shops. If floral-print designs are not quite up your alley try introducing woven gingham checks or stripes.

**clockwise from top left** *Look for toothbrushes with clear perspex handles that reflect the colour theme of the bathroom.*

*Carmer Yellow*
Plascon A14-2

*Constantia*
Plascon BBO 2

*Duckling*
Plascon A14-4

*Monterey*
Plascon A12-4

*Sun Gold*
Plascon A13-5

*Sunset Orange*
Plascon A12-6

1

2

**clockwise from top left**  *Yellow is uplifting and warm, creating glowing interiors.*

*Update existing plain white bedlinen with checked borders and narrow tie details.*

*Display botanical postcards in vertical rows with lengths of jute cording for inexpensive but fun wall hangings. Attach the cord with masking tape or glue and informally tie the loose ends at the top.*

*Make a curtain with a plastic lining and contemporary tab heading for an interesting alternative to ready-made shower curtains. Affix tabs with Velcro to make the curtain easily removable.*

*If you have a bit of time and patience, make a fun project out of transforming existing plain enamel or steel buckets with oil paints.*

*See pages 156 - 157 for fabric details.*

# elements

3

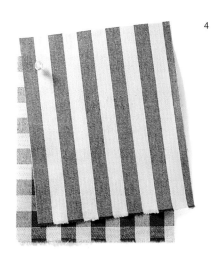

4

5

Bring a feeling of space and light to your surroundings with inspiration from the vibrant colour and relaxed lifestyle of far-flung, sunny places. Absorb the intense azure of the  water, the brilliance of sunlight and the saturated greens of the landscape. Awaken your senses with a delightful simplicity of style – free-form flowers and abstract patterns printed on voiles and cottons, spice coloured canvas fabrics, loose-covered furniture and contemporary accessories create a bright look that is playful and far from ostentatious.

CREATIVE COLOUR

# Sittingroom

Give a twist to traditional floral furnishings by blending stencilled free-form patterns and bright, fresh hues. Strong colours and tactile fabric prints appeal to today's relaxed lifestyle and fit easily into the smaller spaces of modern houses. Contemporary decorating accessories with clean lines and simple shapes are best for this look. Explore ways to maximise the use of space. A good example is the rectangular woven basket with handles – a modern, portable and storable alternative to the traditional magazine rack.

**clockwise from top left**

*Contrast intense bursts of colour with brilliant white and stick to simple furnishings.*
*A small console table in front of a window provides space for reading and writing.*

# Diningroom

Combine contemporary floral prints, distressed white wooden furniture and printed sheers for a refreshingly simple, informal and serene dining area. Coloured and clear crystal glassware adds a touch of opulence to the scheme. Look at antique markets for glassware dating from the Thirties or browse department or chain stores for comparable styles. Sheer tablecloths are unusual, add a sense of lightness and allow the texture of the table to shine through.

**opposite** *Contrast the delicate sheerness of a voile tablecloth with brightly coloured plates to ensure the continuation of the decorating scheme and to add interest and detail.*

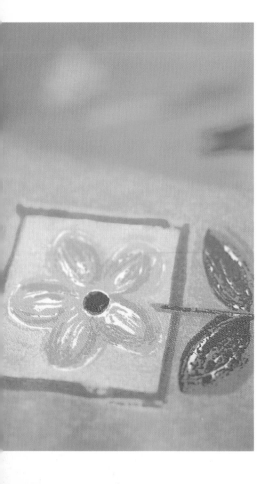

# Kitchen

The homespun appearance of this kitchen is given a modern edge with the use of brilliant blues, greens and yellows. The defined use of strong colour is graphic and picks out key design elements – a bright blue cabinet and door-frame detail and rich mustard loose-covered chair – in an otherwise all-white scheme. To give this look extra zest, use high-lights of contrasting colour such as the luscious lime green throw. Fabric throws are effective decorating tools and also incredibly simple to make. Instead of sliding doors and built-in units hiding away kitchen tools, rather stand glass and ceramic storage jars on top of cabinets or open shelving.

**clockwise from top left** *Free-form floral designs are modern yet traditional.*
*Strong colours require strong flavours. For the most fragrant curry dishes, try making your own curry-paste at home.*
*Easy to reach open storage is efficient and decorative and convenient for dedicated cooks.*

146

# Bedroom

The bedroom is peaceful and serene – everything is selected to hold and reflect light. The walls are covered in textured terracotta wallpaper and kept virtually bare to allow the uninterrupted flow of colour. Pattern only appears as an accent in the plump comforter and cushions. The flowing lines of the paint effect large-scale floral design are echoed in the scalloped flap detail of the cushions. The bed is given a soft touch with a dreamy muslin corona with inverted pleats and tie detail. A similar effect can

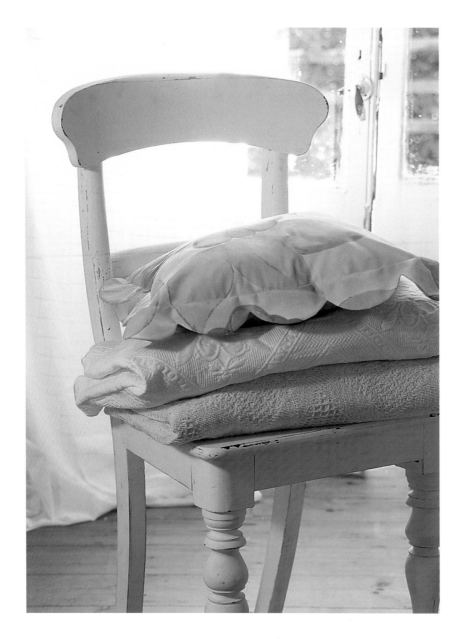

**clockwise from top left** *Bright colours have the most impact when contrasted with white - a combination best suited for sunny climates.*

*The bright colours of nature inspired the use of colour in these fabric designs.*

*Style does not have to be expensive. An inexpensive table wine was sold in this carafe.*

*Fun textured stripe and geometric wallpapers are ideally suited to this look.*

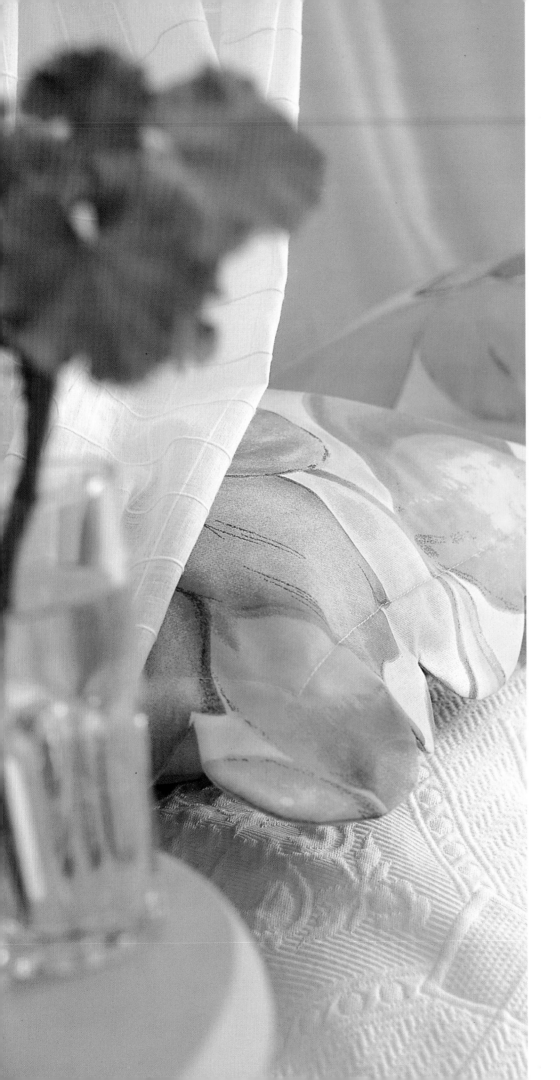

be achieved by loosely draping muslin over the frame of a four poster bed. Loose standing armoires and wardrobes are still the more stylish storage option for clothing, but perhaps not the most practical if space is limited. Nowadays, there is a much wider selection of really good-looking built-in wardrobe units to choose from. If you still can't find anything suitable, commission a reputable carpenter to custom- make a wardrobe, or consider updating an existing unit with contemporary styled doors. Sometimes a simple change – such as replacing the doorknobs – can completely alter the style. Give old trunks a new lease of life with a coat of paint or a textured paint finish. Trunks are always useful to store smaller pieces of clothing or excess bed linen.

# Bathroom

Modern shapes and utility are combined in this bathroom. A backdrop of strong colour holds together a simple, understated blend of steel, wicker and white. The hanging rail system is an innovative and contemporary storage solution – holding towels, toiletries and even decorating accessories. Make sure there is a definite order in the way you put together displays in a system like this, and be sensitive and selective in your choice of toiletries. Look for toothbrushes with beechwood or clear perspex handles, unadorned ceramic toothbrush holders, plain fragrant soaps and bath balls with simple, clear-cut shapes.

**clockwise from top** *Decant products such as day-to-day shampoos and bath oils into clear glass bottles found at most department stores or bath shops. Add a light-hearted touch with accessories such as this decorative boat.*
*Look for laundry baskets with clean and simple lines to compliment this modern style.*

*Maize Field*
Plascon A14-3

*Sunburst*
Plascon A14-5

*Blue Glaze*
Plascon C31-4

*Chagall*
Plascon A31-5

*Clover*
Plascon B22-5

*Dill*
Plascon B22-6

1

2

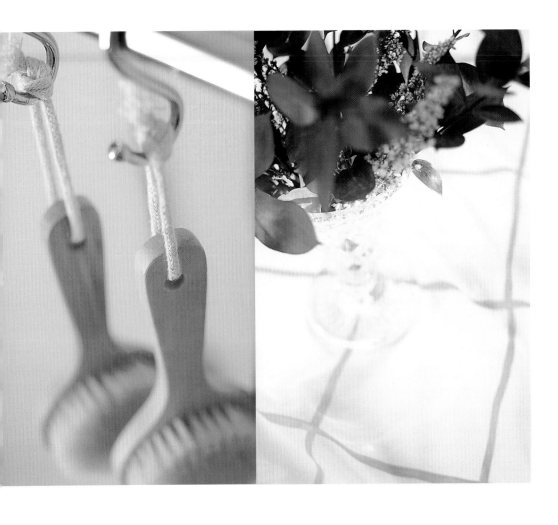

**clockwise from left** *Bright blues, greens and yellows are uplifting and create a warm atmosphere.*

*Look for fabrics with free-form floral and abstract designs and colour-washed textures.*

*Accentuate architectural detailing with bright colour for a graphic effect. You will need: White and blue emulsion paint, masking tape, brushes. Step by step: 1. Repair surface blemishes and apply two coats of white paint. 2. Mask door frame and ledges with masking tape. Rub edges of the tape carefully to secure. 3. Using a narrow brush, paint masked-off areas. Let paint dry before removing the tape.*

*Mix modern brights with natural elements such as light woods, and contrast with steel for a contemporary effect.*

*Create a feeling of lightness by complimenting sheers with clear crystal.*

*See pages 156 - 157 for fabric details*

# e l e m e n t s

3

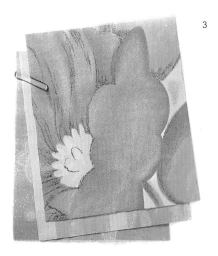

4

5

# Credits

**page 1** yellow glass The Plush Bazaar; tablecloth Voile Trellis Mustard Biggie Best

**page 2** selection of fabrics from the Mediterranean range Biggie Best

**page 3** selection of woven stripes, checks, jacquards and canvas fabrics Biggie Best

**page 4** dried lemons The Bright House

**page 6** curtains in Jute Muslin, pancake cushion cover in Cream Basecloth Biggie Best

**page 9** deckchair cover in Provincial Biggie Best

**page 10** rattan mats The Bright House

**page 11** *clockwise from top left*: cushion with tie detail in Steel Blue Stripe Biggie Best; folded fabrics from the Chateaux Blue and Gold range Biggie Best; scatter cushion with rope and tassel detail Biggie Best; bed cover in Cream Basecloth Biggie Best

**page 12** *top left*: Bristol chair with loose cover in Natural Canvas Biggie Best

**page 13** twig urns Biggie Best

**page 14** pumice Côté Bastide

**page 15** *clockwise from top left*: shower curtain Victorian Bathrooms, frame City Living; cushion Biggie Best; Biggie Best chair with loose cover in Cream Basecloth and runner in Cream Basecloth and Plain Mustard Biggie Best

**page 16** *top left*: tablecloth in Morocco check Biggie Best; *bottom right*: Small Sardinian Check Green Sarah Fleming

**page 20** sofa in Morocco check, fabric drape in Large Navy and Fawn check, chair in Small Candy C check, sofa in foreground in Spain check and selected scatter cushions all Biggie Best

**page 21** selection of scatter cushions and curtains in Biggie Best's range of woven checks.

**page 23** tablecloth in Small Candy B check Biggie Best; antique plates The Plush Bazaar; terracotta pots same at The Plush Bazaar; chairs painted in Plascon Deep Forest B23-7 ; candles The Bright House

**page 24** *top left*: cupboard lined with Small Sardinian Check Blue and Small Sardinian Check Yellow Sarah Fleming

**page 25** *fabric from top to bottom*: Large Navy and Fawn check, Large Candy C check, Small Candy B check all Biggie Best; antique plate and fork The Plush Bazaar

**page 26-27** black wrought iron bed, Terracotta Textural wallpaper, Ecru Jacquard bedspread, Multi-check patchwork quilt, Natural throw, curtain in Morocco check, Oxford pillow and scatter cushion in Small Navy and Fawn check all Biggie Best; brush and mirror set Past and Present

**page 29** alarm clock The Bright House

**page 30-31** toiletries Côté Bastide; Neo Classic basin and pedestal and Long Reach basin taps Victorian Bathrooms

**page 32-33** *pictures from left to right*: tablecloth in Morocco Biggie Best; tablecloth in Small Candy B Biggie Best; distressed pictures Biggie Best; cushion in Spain Biggie Best; *fabric swatches*: 1. Large Navy and Fawn check and Small Navy and Fawn check 2. Spain check and Canvas Blue 3. Large Candy C check, Canvas Dark Mustard and Small Candy B check 4. Morocco and Canvas Brick 5. Green, Burgandy and Fawn check all Biggie Best

**page 34** Brown Canvas Stripe and Brown Textural wallpaper Biggie Best

**page 36** Brown Textural wallpaper, Buckingham Squareback sofa and Victorian Chesterfield chair both in Natural Canvas loose covers, Celton dresser, coffee table, twig urns, scatter cushions and blind in Cream Basecloth all Biggie Best; large white candle The Bright House; side table The Plush Bazaar; side table painted in Plascon Broken White G376

**page 38** knitted cushion cover Biggie Best

**page 39** *clockwise from top left*: Buckingham squareback sofa and scatter cushions Biggie Best; limestone bowls The Bright House; seedballs Biggie Best; candles and limestone flat dish The Bright House; Canvas Stripe Brown and Brown Textural wallpapers Biggie Best

**page 40-41** tablecloth in Cream Basecloth Biggie Best; hurricane lamps and glasses Bric-a-Brac Lane; pasta bowls Continental China

**page 45** cupboard painted in Plascon Frites C15-4; chair painted in Plascon Parmesan A9-2; wall painted in Plascon Paprika WAA 54; mixing bowl Bric-a-Brac Lane; hanging rail and hooks Victorian Bathrooms; throw, cupboard curtain lining in Cream Basecloth all Biggie Best

**page 46-47** canopy, night frill and tablecloth in Cream Basecloth, bolsters in Natural Canvas, Textural Brown wallpaper, Ecru Jacquard bedspread, Tall Lampbase, Jacquard lampshade, Winchester chair in Jacquard loose cover, scatter cushion and White Muslin curtain all Biggie Best

**page 48** *top left*: fabric drape Cream Muslin, wrought iron bed, Ecru Jacquard Bedspread and cushions Biggie Best; Sardinian Small Check Brown comforter Sarah Fleming; *bottom right*: Tall lamp base and Jute Trim lamp shade Biggie Best; frame Graphiti; *bottom left*: Bristol chair with loose cover in Natural Canvas and scatter cushions Biggie Best

**page 49** bed loose cover in Cream Basecloth, Ecru Jacquard bedspread and Natural throws Biggie Best

**page 50-51** curtain in Jute Muslin Biggie Best

**page 52-53** throw and blind in Natural Canvas; Slipper bath, Bath Shower Mixer taps with handset, beech toothbrushes and mugs Victorian Bathrooms; waffle weave towels and soaps Bric-a-Brac Lane; toiletries Côté Bastide; basket The Plush Bazaar

**page 54-55** *pictures from left to right*: Jute Muslin Biggie Best; White Muslin Biggie Best; frame Graphiti; bedcover in Cream Basecloth Biggie Best; *fabric swatches*: 1. Twill Stripe and Twill Check 2. Script Block and Script 3. Natural Canvas 4. Jute Muslin 5. Damask Natural all Biggie Best

**page 58-59** blind in Olivia Tea, Celton table, button footstool in Twill Stripe Cream, Celton cupboard, Leicester sofa with loose cover in Natural Canvas and scatter cushions in Olivia Tea, Odette Tea, Rose and Dot and Olivia Pink and Blue all Biggie Best; round table Sarah Fleming; glass container Bric-a-Brac Lane

**page 60** folded fabric Bramble Rose Biggie Best; old suitcase same at The Plush Bazaar

**page 62** colander, canisters, enamel bucket, antique tea cups and selection of glass containers The Plush Bazaar; blind in Cream basecloth Biggie Best

**page 65** tea-cosy in Ticking Pink, basket lining English Rose Biggie Best

**page 66-67** cushions in Olivia Tea, Odette Tea and Odette Pink and Blue, Ecru Jacquard bedspread and blind in white muslin Biggie Best

**page 68** *top right*: Celton dresser and cream photoframe Biggie Best; *bottom right*: cushions in Olivia Tea and Odette Pink and Blue; *bottom middle*: lamp base Biggie Best; *bottom left*: postcards Graphiti

**page 69** Winchester chair with Olivia Tea loose cover and scatter cushions Biggie Best

**page 70-71** antique bottle The Plush Bazaar; Victorian bath and Chrome Bathrack and Book Rest all Victorian Bathrooms

**page 72-73** *pictures from left to right*: blind in Roses and Ribbons Biggie Best; picture The Plush Bazaar; roses Kenly Flowers; antique cup The Plush Bazaar; *fabric swatches*: 1. Bramble Rose and Ticking Pink 2. Rose and Dot 3. Natural Canvas 4. Olivia Tea and Odette Tea 5. Odette Pink and Green and Olivia Pink and Green all Biggie Best

**page 76-77** curtain in Fleur de Lis white muslin and tablecloth and scatter cushion in Sardinian Wide Stripe Red Sarah Fleming; pictures on mantelpiece and table Graphiti; Winchester chair with loose cover in Twill Check Cream Biggie Best

**page 80** Biggie Best chairs with loose cover in Sarah Fleming Sardinian Small

Check Red; runner in Cream Basecloth and Mini Check Red border Biggie Best; striped tins and decanter The Plush Bazaar; hanging lamp and white ceramic dish The Bright House

**page 82** comforter and curtain tie-backs in Sardinian Large Check Red, lamp base, scatter cushions in Tramline Check Red and gold trim lamp base all Sarah Fleming; bed curtains in Cream Basecloth, button footstool in Twill Stripe Cream and Jute Trim Square lampshade Biggie Best

**page 84** curtains in Small Sardinian Check Red and scatter cushion in Tramline Check Red Sarah Fleming; tie-on cushion in Mini Red Check and Wreath Towels Biggie Best; Cleo bath, Gold Shower Mixer, Gold Soap Dish and Gold Bathrack Victorian Bathrooms; Toiletries Côté Bastide

**page 86-87** *fabric swatches*: 1. Large Sardinian Check Red Sarah Fleming, Twill Check Cream Biggie Best and Small Sardinian Check Red Sarah Fleming 2. Tramline Check Red Sarah Fleming 3. Sardinian Wide Stripe Red Sarah Fleming and Twill stripe Cream Biggie Best 4. Cream Basecloth and Mini Check Red Biggie Best 5. White Muslin Biggie Best

**page 88** antique serving plate The Plush Bazaar; white emboidered napkin Biggie Best

**page 90-91** Barberton daisies Kenly Flowers; curtain and scatter cushions in Floral Delight, straight-back chairs with loose covers in Damask Old Rose and Damask Gold and Winchester Chair with Damask Cream loose cover Biggie Best

**page 92** curtains in Fragrant Appeal with Damask Old Rose centre borders, white embroidered napkins, Celton cupboard, Celton dining table and chairs and tablecloth in Cream Basecloth Biggie Best; flowers Kenly Flowers

**page 94** *clockwise from top left*: white plate Continental China; utensils Bric-a-Brac Lane; antique china The Plush Bazaar; sieve Bric-a-Brac Lane

**page 92** tablecloth in Floral Delight Biggie Best; lamp The Bright House; framed pegboard Graphiti; chairs painted in Plascon Broken White G376; walls painted in Plascon Antique White VEL6

**page 96** curtains in Floral Delight and Cream Basecloth, Floral Delight comforter, frilled pillow cases in Floral Delight, Oxford flap pillow cases in Quisique and Mini Green check, set of sheets with border, Floral Delight pleated lampshades and white Candlestick lampbase all Biggie Best

**page 98** curtains in Floral Delight and Cream Basecloth, scatter cushion in Fragrant Appeal and chair loose cover in Damask Old Rose Biggie Best

## Picture Credits

# Suppliers

## Biggie Best Shops

*There are more than 130 Biggie Best stores worldwide, with more opening on a regular basis.*

### Australia
*Cambeltown,* Hollylea House, 11/85 Airds Road, Leu Meah, NSW 2560, 02-46207350
*Geraldton,* Shop 5, Stirling Centre, WA 6530, 08-99218165
*Griffith,* Shop 4, 26 Ulong Street, NSW 2680, 02-69643559
*Indooroopilly,* Shop 3005, Indooroopilly Shopping Centre, QLD 4068, 07-38784866
*Melbourne,* Shop 10, Pines Shopping Centre, VIC 3109, 03-98417433
*Melbourne,* 216 Canterbury Road, Canterbury, VIC 3126, 03-98884484
*Mittagong,* 107 Main Street, NSW 2575, 02-48712791
*Perth,* 40 Napoleon Street, Cottesloe WA 6010, 08-93853770
*Perth,* Shop 3A, 428 Hay Street, Subiaco, WA 6008, 08-93883070
*Sydney,* 46 Sailors Bay Road, Nortbridge, NSW 2063, 02-99585249
*Wagga Wagga,* 60 Thompson Street, NSW 2650, 02-69218012
*Walkerville,* Shop 3, 70 Walkerville Tce, SA 5081, 08-83447433
*Woolongong,* cnr Stewart & Corrimal Street, NSW 2520, 02-42289644

### Belgium
*Gent,* Brabantdam 15, 09-2341434
*Knokke,* Dumortierlaan 21, 050-622237
*Liege,* Ave Du Centenaire, 24 Embourg, 04-3612747
*Kortrijk,* Broelkaai 10, 056-226755

### Chile
*Concepción,* Cochrane 670, Piso 1, 041-214887
*Santiago,* Alonso de Cordova 2894, 02-2289570
*Santiago,* Av. La Dehesa 1744, 02-2423582

### China
*Shenjen,* 117 Shang Bu South Road, 0755-3206462

### Cyprus
*Nicosia,* Makarious Avenue 54a, 072-420891

### Equador
*Guayaquil,* Urb Alban Borja, Edif, 593-4-203222
*Quito,* Alonso de Torres No 43-02 y, Beck Rollo Edif, El Roble, planta baja, Sector El Bosque, 593-2-265546

### France
*Angers,* 7/9 Rue Louis De Romain, 02-41-209742
*Cannes,* 6 Rue Jean Daumas, 04-93-689011
*Paris,* 1, 9/11 Rue des Lavandieres, 01-40410313
*Rouen,* 18 Rue Jean Lecanuet, 0235-717302
*Toulouse,* 25 Rue Crois-Baragnon, 0561-321000

### Germany
*Bochum,* Westenfelder Strasse 1, 02327-18191
*Mulheim,* Rhein-Ruhr-Zentrum 227, 0208-7820667
*Munich,* Brunnstrasse 7, 089-2605949

### Greece
*Athens,* 14 Solonos Street, Kolonaki, 01-3641727

### Holland
*Amsterdam,* PC Hooftstraat 121, 020-6644022
*Bussum,* Nassaulaan 41-43, 035-6920898
*Maastricht,* Wycker Brugstraat 21A, 043-3255977
*'s-Gravenhage,* Plaats 161, 070-3634040
*s'Hertogenbosch,* Vughterstraat 96, 073-6142117
*Utrecht,* Steenweg 9, 030-2367865

### Hong Kong
*Hong Kong,* Shop 11, G/F, Aberdeen Marina Club Building, 8 Shum Wan Road, Aberdeen, 852-25183448

### Ireland
*Dublin,* Blackrock Shopping Centre, 01-2884822
*Dublin,* 60 Dawson Street, 01-6777077

### Italy
*Bari,* Via Abate Gimma, 32, 080-5235058
*Bergamo,* Via Zelasco 18/c, 035-232702
*Bologna,* Via De' Toschi, 9B, 051-228150
*Cagliari,* Via G Cima, 5/7, 070-653516
*Caserta,* Via Nazionale Appia, 181Casagiove, 0823-466854
*Catania,* Viale Liberta, 095-538185
*Ferrara,* Via San Romano 141, 0532-762013
*Genova,* Via XII Ottobre 112/R, 010-5535127
*Lecce,* Centro Comm. Ipergum S Cesario, 0832-354173
*Livorno,* Viale G Mameli, 43, 0586-806885
*Lucca,* Via Del Battistero, 41, 0583-47776
*Milano,* Corso Magenta, 12, 02-72005250
*Modena,* Corso Canalchiaro, 126, 059-244412
*Napoli,* Piazza San Pasquale, 7, 081-7642527
*Napoli,* Via M. Kerbaker, 33-35, 081-5569555
*Padova,* Via Altinate, 50/52, 049-8753031
*Palermo,* Via Simone Corleo 5, 091-328043
*Pescara,* Via G. Parini, 10/12, 085-4217193
*Reggio,* Calabria Via San Paolo, 1/D, 0965-25936
*Rimini,* Corso D'Augusto 212, 0541-51906
*Roma,* Centro Comm Cinecitta 2, Via Palmiro Togliatti, 06-7213327
*Roma,* Piazza Euclide 3, 06-8072989
*Roma,* Centro Comm I Granai, Via Tazio Nuvolari, 06-51957881
*Roma,* Via Del Corso, 435, 06-6878530
*Salerno,* Via Raffaele Conforti 13/15, 089-225160
*Taranto,* Via Ciro Giovinazzi 5a-5c, 099-4533020
*Torino,* Centro Comm Le "Le Gru" Grugliasco, 011-7708263
*Treviso,* Piazza Duomo 28, 0422-56500
*Udine,* C Via Poscolle, 24, 0432-229684
*Venezia,* C Comm Le "Valecenter" -Marcon-, 041-5951232
*Verona,* Piazza Erbe 3, 045-8002427
*Vicenza,* Piazza Biade 12, 0444-327001

### Kuwait
*Safat,* Salehia Shopping Centre, 054-734177

### Malaysia
*Kuala Lumpur,* 4 Jalan Telawi Lima, Bangsar Baru 603-2840007

### Malta
*Balzan,* Valley Dolphin Shopping Centre, 06-446239

### Namibia
*Swakopmund,* Shop 17, Post Street, 064-402186
*Windhoek,* Garthanri Park, Kelvin Street, 061-228793

### New Zealand
*Auckland,* 1 Cook Street, Howick, 09-5375624
*Auckland,* Shop 5, Remuera Mall 09-5249986
*Christchurch,* Fendalton Village, 240 Clyde Road, 03-3514272
*Dunedin,* 595 Highgate, Maori Hill, 03-4667007
*Nelson,* Shop 1, Robinson Complex, Stoke, 03-5472526
*Wellington,* 326 Tinakori Road, Thorndon, 04-4990475

**Peru**
*Lima,* Jorge Basadre No. 280, San Isidro, 014-4407168
*Lima,* Tiendas A-277 y 228 Centro Comercial El Polo, Av. El Polo No 740, Surco, 014-4344744

**Portugal**
*Cascais,* Rua Alexandre Herculano 20, 011-4846153
*Lisbon,* Mercomar Motores E Acessorio, AV Miguel Bombarda 147b, 011-3525175

**Singapore**
*Singapore,* Tanglin Shopping Centre, 19 Tanglin Rd, 65-2355020 www.danovel.com.

**South Africa**
*Bedfordview,* Bedford Shopping Centre, 011-6153265
*Bloemfontein,* Mimosa Mall, 051-4441863
*Cape Town,* Vineyard Road, Claremont, 021-641590
*Cape Town,* Gardens Shopping Centre, 021-4615454
*Cape Town,* 19C Bella Rosa Street, Rosenpark, 021-9143696
*Durban,* Wakefields Building Berea, 031-2020042
*East London,* Chamberlain Centre, 043-7260482
*Ermelo,* Cnr Kerk & Burger Street, 01781-14836
*George,* Donerail House, 0448-743704
*Johannesburg,* Top Crop Centre, DF Malan Drive, 011-7952895
*Johannesburg,* North K90 Centre, Boksburg North, 011-8231540
*Johannesburg,* Fourways Mall, 011-4651012
*Johannesburg,* Sandton City, 011-7837598
*Johannesburg,* Horizon View Shopping Centre, 011-7637630
*Klerksdorp,* Game Centre, 018-4643139
*Knysna,* Thessen House, 6 Long Street, 044-3823263
*Port Elizabeth,* 39 Pearson Street, Central, 041-564780
*Potchefstroom,* Pick 'n Pay Centre, 018-2978352
*Pretoria,* Atterbury Value Mart, Faerie Glen, 012-9914828
*Rustenburg,* Safari Tuine Complex, 014533-4201

*Somerset West,* Somerset Mall, 021-8523825
*Vereeniging,* 108 General Herzog Road, 016-4235101
*Welkom,* Engko Interiors, Shoprite Centre, 057-3526052
*Witbank,* Highland Mews Shopping Centre, 0136-924625

**South Korea**
*Seoul,* Hyundai Department Store, Samsung-Dong 02-5522233

**Spain**
*Barcelona,* Provenza 266, 93-4874433
*Gijon,* C Langreo No 13, 98-5353449
*Granada,* C Pedro Antoniio De Alarcon 19, 95-8520083
*Gran Canaria,* C Perdomo 7, Las Palmas, 38-92381429
*Madrid,* Velazquez 35, 91-5752716
*Mallorca,* Plaza Del Rosario 3, 971-717708
*Santiago,* C/Montero Rion 46, 981-574597
*Tenerife,* Imeldo Seris 100, Santa Cruz, 922-248228

**Sweden**
*Stockholm,* Kungsgatan 27, 08-4115501

**Switzerland**
*Geneva,* Blvd Georges Favon 9, 022-3101240
*Fribourg,* Rue De Lausanne 34, 026-3231324
*Lugano,* Galleria Central Park, Via Riva Caccia, 091-9932670

**United Kingdom**
*Ballymena,* 21/23 Church Street, Northern Ireland, 01266-632502
*Cheltenham,* 22 Montpellier Walk, 01242-577737
*Hinckley,* Leics 5-7 Windsor Street, Burbage, 01455-615068
*Jersey,* 26 Burrard Street, St Hellier, 01534-632173

## Biggie Best Warehouses

*For franchise information contact one of the international offices.*

**Australia**
20 Graylands Road, Claremont, Perth
Tel: +61-89-3834155
Fax: +61-89-3852140
e-mail: bigibest@upnaway.com

**South Africa**
1 Fir Street, Observatory, Cape Town
Tel: +27-21-4481264
Fax: +27-21-4487057
e-mail: bigibest@global.co.za

**United Kingdom**
109 South Liberty Lane, Bristol
Tel: +44-117-9872722
Fax: +44-117-9872744
e-mail:biggie-best@cableinet.co.uk

## Fabric

**Sarah Fleming**
Available from selected Biggie Best shops and other decor shops
1 Fir Street, Cape Town
Tel: +27-21-4481966
Fax: +27-21-472921

## Flowers

**Kenly Flowers**
Sir Lowry Road, Woodstock, Cape Town
Tel: +27-21-4619140
Fax: +27-21-4619393

## Kitchens and bathrooms

*Ideas for fittings and accessories:*

**House & Interiors at Bric-a-Brac Lane**
Corwen Street , Claremont, Cape Town  Tel: +27-21-6831468
Fax: +27-21-6833314

**Bright House**
Shop L41, Cavendish Square, Claremont, Cape Town
Tel: +27-21-6836012
97 Bree Street, Cape Town
Tel: +27-21-249024

**Continental China**
Wholesale: Range Road, Blackheath TA Cochina, Cape Town
Tel: +27-21-9051120
Fax: +27-21-9051811
Factory Shop: Range Road, CT
Tel: +27-21-9051120

**City Living**
Buitenkloof Centre, 8 Kloof Street, Cape Town
Tel: +27-21-249424

**Victorian Bathrooms**
*Head office:* 144 Wetton Road, Wetton, Cape Town
Tel: +27-21-7042340
Fax: +27-21-7041366
*Showroom:* 13 Corwen Street, Claremont, Cape Town
Tel/Fax: +27-21-6834756
e-mail: vicbaths@iafrica.com

## Pictures and frames

**Graphiti Picture Framers**
83 Long Street, Cape Town
Tel: +27-21-4238491

## Second hand

**Past and Present**
127 Long Street, Cape Town
Tel: +27-21-4230861

**The Plush Bazaar**
30 Somerset Road, Cape Town
Tel/Fax: +27-21-4198328

## Paint

**Plascon**
Advisory service
Tel: 0860204060 (RSA nation-wide)

## Workshops

**Miss Lyn**
Cushions, loose covers and other soft furnishings
Fir Street, Observatory, Cape Town
Tel: +27-21-4473419

**Naomi Hendriks**
Curtains, blinds, cushions, and other soft furnishings
5 Crete Road, Wetton, Cape Town
Tel: +27-21-7618109
Fax: +27-21-7618173

**NOTE**
Specific product featured in this book may not be available from the various stores at all times. Similar product lines should however be available.

# acknowledgements

Firstly, thank you to Biggie Best International, in particular to owner Pru Pfuhl, for believing in this project and for providing unconditional support and encouragement. My thanks also to everyone at Biggie Best who have been so helpful and patient with endless requests for products and information. A huge thank you to photographer Craig Fraser for his stunning descriptive images, enthusiasm, dedication and good humour. Many thanks to Holger Schutt who energetically assisted me on numerous shoots; to Ellen Fitz-Patrick for her knowledgeable editing of my text; to old colleague and dear friend Tina-Marié Malherbe for sharing her design expertise; and to all the crafts-people involved in the soft furnishings, wallpapering and decorative painting. I must also express my gratitude to Victorian Bathrooms, Graphiti and Plascon for generously supplying products and fulfilling special requests without flinching. Thanks to my mother and father for their interest and encouragement, and above all, a big thank you to my wonderfully supportive husband Ben and our adorable baby boy, Thinus, for putting up with my too frequent absences over the past few months.